The Christmas Story

Told In All Seasons

To Be Read Aloud
Parents to Children / Children to Parents
Grandparents to Grandchildren / Grandchildren to Grandparents
Children to Children
You to Friends and Enemies

GREG GARR

Xulon PRESS

PREFACE

I tell my daughters, "I'm just another voice, not so much a voice crying in the wilderness, but to a nation of believers and those who will come to follow Christ." "The Christmas Story Told In All Seasons" (to be read aloud) is an effort to give a nation a tool to accomplish the task of introducing-- through simplicity and rhyme--Jesus Christ to all who read and hear. This work is meant to be read aloud to the rhythm of the Christmas story, "Twas The Night Before Christmas." The book opens with a pregnant Mary on a donkey and Joseph traveling to Jerusalem to be counted for the census, to Christ's birth, to prominent stories of Jesus' miracles and teaching, to Christ's crucifixion, burial, resurrection, ascension, and the beginning of the church as we know it today. I want to say again, I'm just another voice, but I am a voice, and it is the voices of all Christ's followers who are needed to lead our nation back to God and our savior Jesus Christ.

INDEX TO CAST OF CHARACTERS

1. Jesus of Nazareth
2. Bartimaeus – The Blind Beggar
3. Jesus – 12 Years Old
4. Martha
5. Samaritan Woman
6. Joseph – Husband of Mary
7. Mary – Mother of Jesus
8. Wise Men
9. Mary Magdalene
10. Thomas
11. Mary – Annoints Jesus' Feet
12. Lazarus
13. Caiaphas
14. Joseph of Arimathea
15. Centurian
16. Zacchaeus
17. Peter
18. James
19. Judas
20. Pontius Pilate
21. John
22. Nicodemus
23. Matthew
24. An Angel
25. Holy Spirit
26. Angel
27. Baby Jesus
28. John the Baptist
29. Christ on Cross

TABLE OF CONTENTS

CHAPTER 1
JESUS

Just days before Christ's birth, and all through the land,
Census was taken, of each woman and man.

Mary was pregnant, and about to give birth,
To a child who was promised, to save us on earth.

The donkey was packed, and ready to ride,
Mary atop, and Joseph aside.

The shepherds were on the hillside, grazing their sheep,
When out of the heavens, the angels did speak.

The angels began to sing aloud, "Glory to God in the highest,
Peace on earth, to those on whom His favor rest.

"Fear not; I bring you tidings of great joy,
About the birth, of a little boy.

"For unto you a child, will be born this day;
To lead and guide us, in all our ways.

"And this, shall be a sign,
A babe, wrapped in swaddling clothes, you'll find,

"Lying, in a manger,
Warm, and safe from danger."

When all the angels there, had left them,
The shepherds said, "Let us go to Bethlehem,

"And see the things, that have come to pass,
Which the Lord has made known, to us at last."

Mary and Joseph, came from Nazareth to Bethlehem,
And found, there was no room in the inn.

This child "Jesus," a babe lying in a manger,
Wonderful, Counselor--the Everlasting Father.

And when the shepherds had seen Him, they spread the word,
All were amazed, at what they heard.

It was spread abroad, what had come to pass,
The Messiah who was prophesied, had come at last.

But Mary treasured these things, and pondered them in her heart,
And the shepherds glorify, and praise God as they depart.

Now the visit of the wise men came, months after Jesus' birth,
With gifts for Him from afar--gold, frankincense, and myrrh.

On the day of purification, He was offered to God by Simeon,
And the child was named Jesus, the name the angels gave Him.

His name was announced, before He was conceived,
This had happened six times before, you see.

There was Ishmael, Isaac, Solomon, and Josiah,
Cyrus a king, and John the Baptist, son of Zachariah.

Simeon took Him in his arms, and raised Him to God,
Saying, "My eyes have seen our salvation, salvation for all."

Jesus was left in Jerusalem at twelve, we learn,
Mary and Joseph found Him teaching in the temple, when they returned.

Jesus--listening and answering--all were amazed,
"Of all His teaching and wisdom," they all said.

Mary said, "Why have you treated us like this?
We searched, your father and I, you were greatly missed."

"Why were you searching for me?" He asked,
"Did you not know, I'd be in my Father's house?"

CHAPTER 2
JOHN THE BAPTIST

In the fifteenth year, of the reign of Tiberius Caesar,
When Pontius Pilate, was governor of Judea.

When Herod, was tetrarch of Galilee,
His brothers, were tetrarch of Iturea and Abilene.

During the priesthood of Annas, and Caiaphas,
The word of God came to John, son of Zacharias.

John the Baptist preached, repent of your sins,
In all the country around Jordan, again and again.

They asked, if he was the Messiah.
He replied, "No! You should look for another.

"For I will baptize you with water," he said to the crowd,
"But He will baptize you, with the Holy Spirit and fire."

When John baptized Jesus, Jesus was praying,
Heaven opened up, and the Holy Spirit descending,

And a voice came from Heaven, proclaiming you see,
"You are my Son, whom I love; with You I am well pleased."

Jesus--full of the Holy Spirit returned from the Jordan--
Led by the Spirit, ate nothing and tempted by Satan.

And when the devil had ended, all the temptations,
He departed from Jesus, for the rest of the season.

Jesus went to Galilee, where He was brought up,
On the day of the Sabbath, in the synagogue He taught.

Calling His disciples, in Galilee,
Making them fisher of men, said, "Follow me."

Jesus called his disciples by one, some by two,
Andrew and Peter, Philip, and Nathanael, too.

CHAPTER 3
THE WEDDING FEAST

In Cana of Galilee at the wedding feast, the wine ran out,
Mary the mother of Jesus knew what to do, no doubt.

Jesus said, "Woman, what does your concern have to do with me?"
His mother said to the servant, "Whatever He says, do it you see."

Now the wine was all gone,
There sat six water pots of stone.

Fill the water pots for them,
And fill the water pots to the brim.

Then He told them, "Now draw some out,
And take it to the master, of the house."

When the master of the feast, had tasted the wine,
He said, "They saved the best for the last, this wine is divine."

The servant who had drawn the wine knew,
The master of the feast called the bridegroom.

The first miracle Jesus did, in Cana of Galilee,
Manifested His glory, and His disciples believed.

CHAPTER 4
THE PASSOVER

Now the Passover of the Jews, was at hand,
And Jesus went up, to Jerusalem.

In the temple court, He found men selling doves, cattle and sheep,
And others sitting at tables, exchanging money for their profit.

So He made a whip, out of small cords,
And drove men, and cattle, and sheep out the door.

Then the Jews responded, "What authority do you have to act this way?"
Jesus answered, "Destroy this temple, and I will raise it up in three days."

Then the Jews replied, "It was forty-six years in building this sanctuary."
But Jesus spoke of the temple, which is His body.

CHAPTER 5
NICODEMUS

Now there was a Pharisee named Nicodemus--a ruler of the Jews,
This man came to Jesus by night, not knowing what to do.

Said to Jesus, "Rabbi, we know who thou art,
A teacher come from God, no doubt."

In reply Jesus declared, "I tell you my friend,
No one can enter the kingdom of God, unless he's born again."

CHAPTER 6
THE SAMARITAN WOMAN

Now the Pharisees heard, that Jesus was baptizing and discipling,
More followers, than John was gaining.

When the Lord learned of this, He left Judea,
And came to Sychar, a town in Samaria.

To a part of ground,
Where Jacob's well was found.

There came a woman of Samaria to draw water,
It was just about the noon hour.

Jesus said to her, "Give me a drink,"
For His disciples had gone off into town, to buy meat.

The Samaritan woman--a bit puzzled said to Him,
"You are a Jew, and I am a Samaritan woman.

"How can You ask me, for a drink,
For the Jews do not associate with us, like this?"

Jesus answered, "If you had only known, and recognized God's gift,
And who this is saying, to give me a drink.

"You would have asked Him, farther,
And He would have given you, living water."

"Sir", the woman said, "the well is deep, and you have nothing with which to draw,
Where can I get, this living water?"

Jesus answered, "He who drinks this water, will thirst again,
But not if he drinks the water, I have given him."

Jesus said to her, "Go call your husband and come here."
"I have no husband," the woman answered.

Jesus said to her, "You have spoken truly in saying,
That I have no husband, the truth you have spoken.

"For you have had five husbands,
And the one you are now with is not one of them."

"I can see you are a prophet," she said to Him,
"Our fathers worshiped on this mountain, but your people in Jerusalem."

The woman said, "I know He is coming, the Messiah called Christ,
When He comes, He will explain everything to us."

Then Jesus said, "You see,
I who speak to you, am He."

Just then His disciples returned, and wondered,
Why is He talking to this, Samaritan woman?

Then the woman left her water jars, and went to the village,
Said to the men, "Come see a man who told me, everything I ever did."

Many of the Samaritans from the town believed,
In Him because of the woman's testimony.

And He stayed there, for two more days,
Many more believed, because of what He said.

They said to the woman,
From whom truth was spoken.

"Now we have heard, for ourselves,
And we know now, that He is truly our Savior."

CHAPTER 7
ZACCHAEUS

In Jericho, there was a man, by the name of Zacchaeus,
He was a chief tax collector, wealthy, and short of statue.

Zacchaeus was there, and could not see,
So up he climbed, into the Sycamore tree.

When Jesus, reached that spot,
Zacchaeus, was in the tree top.

Jesus looked up, and called to him,
"Zacchaeus, hurry, come down, and be my friend."

Jesus said, "I must stay at your house today,"
So Zacchaeus, came down at once and welcomed him gladly.

And when the people saw that, they all grumbled and mummered,
Saying, "Jesus is going to be guest, of a man who is a sinner."

But Zacchaeus stood up, and said to the Lord,
"Behold, Lord! The half of my goods, I give to the poor.

"And if I have cheated anybody, out of anything,
I give back four times as much, as I have taken."

And Jesus said to him, "Today salvation has come to this house,
For the Son of Man came, to seek, and to save, that which was lost."

CHAPTER 8
BARTIMAEUS

When Jesus and His disciples, were leaving Jericho,
There was a blind beggar man, sitting by the road.

They told him Jesus of Nazareth, was passing by,
The one they heard healed the sick, and opened blind eyes.

As the crowd neared following Jesus, of Nazareth,
"Jesus, Son of David, have mercy on me," Bartimaeus
shouted.

Many rebuked him, and told him to be quiet,
But he shouted the more, to Jesus of Nazareth.

He shouted again, "Son of David, have mercy of me!"
His disciples said, "On your feet, Jesus is calling thee."

And casting aside his cloak,
Jumped to his feet and came to Jesus.

Jesus asked Bartimaeus, "What do you want of me?"
Blind Bartimaeus said, "Rabbi, that I might see."

"Go!" Jesus said, "Your faith has healed you."
Immediately, He received his sight, and followed Jesus.

CHAPTER 9
AS LITTLE CHILDREN

The sons of Zebedee, James and John his brother,
Came to Jesus, with their mother.

"Teacher, in Your glory" they asked,
"Can one sit on Your right, and the other on Your left?"

Jesus replied, "You do not realize,
What you are asking of Me?

"Are you able to drink,
The cup I am about to drink?

"And to be baptized with,
The baptism I am baptized with?"

The ten apostles became indignant, with the others,
When they heard the words, of their brothers.

Then Jesus overturned, the value structure of the world,
And explained the humble and loving, service of a disciple.

For even Christ, did not come to be served,
But to give His life, as a ransom and to serve.

Sitting down with the twelve,
Jesus called, "If anyone wishes to be the first, he must be servant to all."

Jesus took a little child, and had him stand among them,
Taking him in His arms, He said to them,

"Who ever welcomes one of these little children in My name, welcomes me,
And whoever welcomes Me, does not welcome Me, but the One who sent
Me."

CHAPTER 10
MIRACLES

Peter walked on the water, to go to Jesus, and started sinking,
But it was the disciples, in the boat, who were drifting.

Jesus, turned water into wine in Cana,
Healed a demonic, in the synagogue in Capernaum.

A draught of fish, that broke the net in Galilee,
On the same lake, Peter walked with Thee.

In Galilee, the demonic healed,
On the Galilee Sea, the tempest was stilled.

In Capernaum, Jairus' daughter is raised,
And a woman, with an issue of blood gives praise.

A blind man is cured, and a dumb spirit cast out,
This is Jesus the Christ, no doubt.

A widow's son, raised from the dead,
The popularity, of Jesus spread.

He would feed five thousand once, then feed four thousand more;
Some came for the miracles and teaching, some for the fishes and loaves.

One time twelve baskets remained, the other time seven,
He taught of life forever in hell, or forever in heaven.

Ten lepers cleansed, and the one who returned to give thanks
was made whole,
In Caesarea, the devil was cast out of the little boy.

Jesus passed through the crowd, a number of times,
In Jericho two men receive sight, who were blind.

Jesus said, "I and my Father are one,"
For that, the Jews tried to kill Him, they took up stones.

They sought to take Him, again and again,
But he would escape, passing through their hands.

He went away again, beyond Jordan I'm told,
Where John had first baptized, and there he abode.

CHAPTER 11
LAZARUS AND THE GRAVE

Now a man named Lazarus, lay sick in Bethany,
The village of Martha, and her sister Mary.

This Mary was the same one, who poured perfume on the Lord,
And wiped His feet with her hair; it was Martha who sent word.

"Lord, the one you love is sick, and in a bad way,"
When Jesus heard this, He abode for two more days.

Then when Jesus came, He heard he was lain,
In the tomb four days, in Bethany near Jerusalem.

When Jesus saw Mary, Martha, and all others weeping,
He was moved in the Spirit, and troubled and asked, "Where have you laid him?"

"Come see Lord," they replied.
Jesus wept, He who open blind eyes.

Jesus once more deeply moved, came to the cave,
A stone lay upon it--it covered the grave.

"Take away the stone," Jesus said.
Martha replied, "he is four days dead."

Then Jesus said, "Did I not tell you, that if you believed,
The glory of God, you and others would see?"

Then they took away the stone, from the place where the dead man laid,
And Jesus lifted up His eyes to Heaven to God, and said.

"Father, I thank thee, that You hear Me,
So the glory of God, you and others will see."

When He had said this, Jesus called, with a loud voice,
"Lazarus! Lazarus! Lazarus! Come forth."

Lazarus came forth, bound hand to foot in grave clothes,
Jesus said to them, "Take off the linen cloth, loose him, and let him go."

Many Jews who came with Mary, put faith in Him,
But the chief priests and Pharisees, called together the Sanhedrin.

"What shall we do?" the council said,
"Jesus is performing miracles, that man Lazarus, was dead."

CHAPTER 12
JESUS' DEATH PROPHESIED

Caiaphas that year, prophesied,
That for the Jewish nation, Jesus would die.

Not only, for that nation,
But also, God's scattered children.

So from that day on,
A plot to kill Jesus had begun.

The Jewish Passover, was nigh at hand,
And many went out of the country, up to Jerusalem.

Both the chief priests and Pharisees, had given the command,
That if you see Jesus, tell us, let us know, as soon as you can.

CHAPTER 13
MARY ANOINTING JESUS' FEET

There was made a supper,
The one who served was Martha.

And Lazarus, was one of them,
That sat at the table, with Him.

Then Mary anointed Jesus' feet, with a pound of perfume,
Wiped His feet with her hair, its scent filled the room.

But one of the disciples, Judas Iscariot, who would betray Him,
Said, "Why was this not sold, and to the poor given?"

He did not say this because he cared for the poor, he was a thief;
He would help himself to the bag, and to the money put in it.

CHAPTER 14
JESUS' TRIUMPHANT ENTRY INTO JERUSALEM

The next day, the great multitude that had come,
Heard that Jesus, was on His way to Jerusalem.

Jesus sent two of His disciples, for a donkey and a colt,
Those who were with Him, on the colt put a cloak.

Then Jesus sat on the young colt, to fulfill what is written,
"Do not be afraid, O' Daughter of Zion.

"See your kingdom is coming, seated on a donkey's colt,"
Always remember, this triumphant entry you've been told.

As Jesus came, they spread their cloaks on the road,
Cut trees and palm branches, on the road they strowed.

"Hosanna, blessed is He who comes, in the name of the Lord,"
Many who shouted were there, when Jesus called Lazarus forth.

Now there were some Greeks,
Among those at the feast.

They came to Philip, who was from Bethsaida,
"With a request to see Jesus," they said.

Jesus replied, "The hour has come for the Son of Man, to be glorified,
Unless a kernel of wheat, falls to the ground and dies.

"A single seed it remains, no hope for any gain,
But if it dies, it produces many seeds, and eternal life, to those, who
follow Me."

CHAPTER 15
THE LAST SUPPER

Now, before the Passover feast began,
Jesus, knew the time was at hand.

The evening meal was being served, and the devil prompted
Judas Iscariot,
The son of Simon, to betray the Christ Jesus.

Jesus got up from the meal, and laid aside His garment,
And took a towel, and girded Himself with it.

Then He poured water into a basin,
And began to wash the feet of them.

And to wipe them with the towel, with which he was girded,
And so He came to His disciple, Simon Peter.

Peter, said to Him,
"Lord, are you going to wash my feet, as you did them?"

Jesus replied, and answered, and said to him,
"You do not realize now, but later you will understand."

"No!" said Peter, "You shall never wash my feet,"
Jesus answered, "Unless I wash you, you will have no part of me."

"Then Lord," Simon Peter said,
"Not just my feet, but my hands and my head."

Then Jesus said, "He who shares my bread, has lifted up his heel against Me,
I tell you now, so when it happens, you will believe I am He."

After He said this, Jesus was troubled in the spirit,
They stared at one another, at loss of what it meant.

One of them, the disciple whom Jesus loves, was reclining on Him,
Simon Peter, motioned to this disciple, and said, "Ask Him which one He means."

Leaning back against Jesus he asked, "Lord who is it?"
Jesus answered, "It is the one to whom I will give this piece of bread,
after I have dipped it."

Then, dipping the bread in the dish, He gave it to the one who would betray.
As soon as Judas had taken the piece of bread, into him entered Satan,
he was on his way.

Now Judas Iscariot, one of the twelve, went to the priests and Pharisees,
He agreed to betray Him for money, so Judas Iscariot sought an opportunity.

To hand over the teacher of the law,
To them, the priests, and the guard.

When no crowd was present, so there would not be a riot,
This was all set up, by Judas Iscariot.

At supper that night,
Jesus said, "I am the light."

Doubting Thomas would say,
"Lord, how will we know the way?"

Jesus answered, "I am the way, the truth and the life, you see,
No one comes to the Father, but by Me."

That night Jesus would predict Peter's denial,
And takes time to comfort His disciples.

Jesus crossed the Kidron Valley, in the olive grove,
The place where Judas, would always know to go.

Jesus, would pray for all His believers,
Just moments, before He was delivered.

Now the betrayer had arranged a signal, with them,
The one I kiss, is the man Jesus, arrest Him.

Jesus asked them, "Who is it you want?"
And they replied, "Jesus of Nazareth."

Then Simon Peter, who had a sword, drew it,
Cutting off the ear, of the high priest's servant, (Malchus).

Jesus commanded Peter, "Put your sword away,
Shall I not drink the cup, the Father, has given Me this day?"

Then comes one, two, three denials, by Peter,
And Jesus to the Sanhedrin, is delivered.

Then Judas, His betrayer, seeing that Jesus had been condemned and showed remorse,
Brought back the thirty pieces of silver to the chief priests, and elders, and threw them in the court.

CHAPTER 16
TRIAL, SENTENCE, AND CRUCIFIXION

Jesus had been to the Sanhedrin, Annas, and Caiaphas,
Now He was brought before Pilate, to Herod, and back to Pilate.

Pilate would ask, "Are you the King of the Jews?"
Later he would ask, to tell him, "What is truth?"

Pilate said to them, "What shall I do with Jesus, who is called Christ?"
They all cried to him, "Let Him be crucified."

Then the governor said, "Why, what evil is he tried?"
But they all cried out the louder, "Let Him be crucified!"

Pilate washed his hands saying, "I am innocent of the blood of this person,"
Then all the people said, "Let His blood be on us and on our children."

It was customary, to release, a prisoner at the Feast,
And with that, the crowd called, to free Barabbas, and condemned Jesus.

Then the soldiers of the governor took Jesus, I'm told,
And stripped Him of His garment, and put on Him, a scarlet robe.

And they plaited a crown of thorns, and put it on His head,
Put a reed in His right hand, knelt before Him and said.

"Hail King of the Jews!" Then they spit upon Him,
Took the reed, and smote Him on His head, again and again.

After they had mocked Him, they took off the scarlet robe,
And put back on Him, His own clothes.

Then they led him away, to be crucified,
But little did they know, to this, He is glorified.

And as they went out,
They forced a man from Cyrene, Simon to carry the cross.

To the place of the skull, called Golgotha, in Hebrew,
Over it a placard that read, "Jesus of Nazareth King of the Jews."

And there were also two other criminals, led with Him to be put to death,
One criminal on His right, and the other criminal on His left.

So again, the scripture was fulfilled,
He was numbered with His transgressors, here on Calvary Hill.

Sitting down, they kept watch over Him there,
And they could see over His head; the accusation that read,

In Latin, and Greek, and Hebrew,
"Jesus of Nazareth, King of the Jews."

Remember, Adam and Eve sinned, and realized they were naked,
Covered themselves with fig leaves, and hid from God in the garden.

God made the first sacrifice, to clothe Adam and Eve with skins,
Jesus now is offering Himself--His blood--for our trespasses and sins.

It was likely lambs you know, Jesus is called, the Lamb of God,
His blood, His life, is now being offered; He is the Christ our Savior.

Jesus cried, "I thirst,"
To be crucified, was the worst.

"Father forgive them, for they know not what they do," Jesus said,
The Christmas Story of Christ, being the final sacrifice, is read.

Near the cross of Jesus, stood His mother,
Mary, the wife of Clopas, Mary Magdalene and His brother.

When Jesus saw, His mother there,
And His disciple who he loved, standing near.

Jesus said to His mother, "Woman behold your son,"
To John He said, "Here is your mother from this time on."

They parted His raiments,
And cast lots for His garment.

Casting lots upon them,
To see which man would win.

And they that passed by railed on Him wagging their heads, they would say,
"Thou that destroy the temple, and will build it back, in three days.

"Save thyself, if you're the most,
And come down, from the cross."

The chief priests, and the teachers, mocked Him the same day,
"He saved others," they said, "But Himself, He cannot save."

"Let this Christ, the King of Israel you see.
Come down now from the cross, that we may see and believe."

At the sixth hour, darkness came over the whole land,
On the ninth hour, Jesus cried out as a man.

"Eloi, Eloi, Lama sa bactha ni,
My God, my God, why have you forsaken me?"

When some of those standing near, heard this,
"Listen, listen, He's calling for the prophet, Elijah."

Jesus cried, "It is finished,"
With that, He bowed His head, and gave up His spirit.

With a loud voice, He cried,
Breathed His last breath, and died.

And the veil of the temple, was rent in twain,
From the top of the veil, to the veil's very bottom.

Now some women at the cross, from a distance you could see,
Mary Magdalene, Mary mother of James (the less), Joses, and Salome.

And when the centurion saw, Jesus cry out,
He said, "Truly, this man was the Son of God, no doubt."

CHAPTER 17
PREPARATION DAY

Now, it was the Day of Preparation,
The next day, was to be a Sabbath celebration.

The bodies could not remain on the cross, on Sabbath day,
They besought Pilate to break their legs, that they might be taken away.

But when they came to Jesus, and found He was already dead,
One of the soldiers, pierced the Christ in the side with a spear.

And a soldier saw it – the eyewitness,
Gives testimony, and this evidence.

He knows, that he tells the truth you see,
So that you may also believe.

For these things came to pass,
It was written in the past.

Not a bone shall be broken,
Of Christ it was spoken.

And again, another scripture reads,
"They shall look on Him, of whom they pierced."

Then came Joseph of Arimathea, to beg the body of Jesus,
But secretly for fear of the Jews, because he was a Jew too.

With Pilate's permission he came,
And took the body of Jesus away.

He was accompanied, by Nicodemus,
The one who first came by night, to Jesus.

Nicodemus, brought for Jesus' burial,
A seventy-five pound mixture; of aloe and myrrh.

Taking Jesus' body, the two of them,
Sprinkled spices, and wrapped it, with strips of linen.

Outside the Jerusalem wall, where Jesus was crucified,
There's a garden and a new family tomb, where no one had been laid.

Time was short; it was Preparation Day,
Since the tomb was nearby, there Jesus was laid.

It was Joseph of Arimathea's tomb, he had hewn out of a rock,
They rolled a great stone to the door of the sepulcher, to then depart.

And Mary Magdalene, and Mary the mother of Joses beheld,
Where, when, and how, He was laid.

Now the next day that followed, the Day of Preparation,
The chief priests and the Pharisees came together to Pilate, for a session.

Saying "Sir, we remember that the deceiver said, while He was yet alive,
'After three days, I will arise.'

"So command the tomb, to be made sure for three days,
Lest His disciple come by night, and take the body away.

"And tell the people, 'He has risen from the dead,'
So the last error shall be worse than the first," they said.

They made the tomb secure, by sealing the boulder,
And commanded a watch--a guard of soldiers.

The women left, and prepared spices and ointments,
And rested the Sabbath day, according to the commandment.

CHAPTER 18
HE IS RISEN

Now on the first day of the week, very early in the morning,
Mary Magdalene, and Salome, and the others came with them.

Asking, "Who will roll away, the stone for us?
We have brought spices and oils, to anoint Jesus."

But when they looked up, they saw the stone rolled away,
They had not come to know, it was Resurrection Day.

And it happened, as they were greatly perplexed about this,
That behold, two men stood by them, in shining garments.

They were afraid, and bowed their faces to the earth, the angel said,
"Why do you seek the living, from the dead?

"He is not here, He is risen,
Remember what He said, while He was still living.

"Remember, He said, He would be crucified,
And then on the third day, His temple, His body would rise."

For as yet they did not know, the scripture said,
That "He must rise again, from the dead."

Now when Jesus arose, on the first day of the week,
He appeared to Mary Magdalene, out of whom seven demons were sent.

She went and told them, "Jesus lives,"
Understanding her every word, yet they did not believe.

While they were on their way, some of the guards,
Reported to the chief priests, all that occurred.

And when they had assembled, with the elders,
And consulted with them, all together,

They gave the soldiers a large sum of money, for a bribe,
Say, "His disciples came by night and stole Him away, while you were
asleep, the truth, we will hide.

"And if this should come, to the governor's ear,
We will persuade him, and make you safe and secure."

And they took the money, and followed their instruction,
And to this day the story, is wide spread among them.

And the eleven disciples, to Galilee proceeded,
To the mountain, where Jesus had designated.

CHAPTER 19
THE ROAD TO EMMAUS

Two of them went that same day, to Emmaus,
And spoke of the things that had happened, to Jesus.

And while they were conversing, and discussing Him,
Jesus approached, and began to travel with them.

But their eyes, were kept from seeing,
The One, in whom, they were believing.

Jesus asked them, "What is this discussion you have,
As the two of you walk and are sad?"

Then one of them named Cleopas, answered Him,
"Are you only a stranger, in Jerusalem,

"Not to know the things, that occurred,
To the One, who spoke the Word?"

"What things," Jesus asked?
They replied, "About Jesus, of Nazareth.

"Who was a prophet, mighty in deed and word,
How is it, that you haven't heard?

"The chief priests, and our rulers, handed Him over to be sentenced.
He was put to trial, He was crucified, and cried 'It is finished.'

"But we were hoping it was He,
Who would redeem and set Israel free.

"And besides all this, now we stand confused and amazed,
At what the women said, that came from the grave after three days.

" 'We did not find the body,' they were saying,
And seen a vision of angels that said, 'He is risen.'

"So Peter and John, and some of those who were with us,
Ran to the tomb, to find Jesus.

"And found it just as the women said,
Jesus was not there, who was dead."

And Jesus said to them, "O foolish ones sluggish of mind and perception,
To believe in all the prophets, and all they have spoken."

Jesus said, "Ought not Christ these things suffered,
And into his Glory He entered."

And through all the prophets, beginning at Moses,
He explained all the scripture, concerning Himself.

Then they drew near to the village,
Jesus acted as if He would go further.

But they urged, and insisted Him saying,
"Stay with us, for it is toward evening."

To that He went in,
To tarry with them.

And it came to pass, as He sat at meat with them,
He took the loaf of bread, and praised God, and gave thanks, and asked
a blessing.

Then Jesus broke the loaf, and was giving it to them.
When their eyes were instantly opened, and they clearly recognized Him.

And He disappeared, from their sight,
They knew surely, it was the Christ.

CHAPTER 20
DOUBTING THOMAS

And they arose that very hour, and returned to Jerusalem,
There they found the disciples of Jesus, with the eleven.

And saying, "The Lord has risen,
And has appeared to Simon."

And they began to relate their experience, on the road,
And how He was revealed to them, in breaking the loaf.

And while they were telling these things, He Himself stood in their midst,
They were startled, and frightened, and thought that they were seeing a spirit.

Jesus said, "Why are you troubled and doubts arise?
Behold, My hands and My feet, it is I."

And when He had spoken, He showed them His hands, and His feet,
And while they were yet to believe, He said, "Have you any meat?"

And they gave Him a piece of broiled fish,
And before them He took it and ate it.

He reminded them that everything must be fulfilled, that is written,
In the Law of Moses, the prophets, and Psalms, concerning Him.

Jesus appeared to one or two of the apostles, it is written,
Sometimes ten, when Thomas was missing.

Jesus appeared to the eleven, while they were eating,
He rebuked them for their lack of faith, and refusal of believing.

Thomas would doubt, "Lord only if I touch your hands and your feet,"
Jesus encouragingly replied, "Thomas handle me and see."

And Jesus would ask Peter, "Lovest thou me more than these?"
By the third time Jesus pressed the issue, Peter grieved.

And said, "You know all things, you know I love thee,"
Jesus replied the third time, "Feed my sheep."

Jesus appeared to James with the other apostles,
And at one time to five hundred disciples.

So when they met together, they asked the Lord,
"Lord, are you at this time going to restore, the Kingdom to Israel?"

Jesus replied, "There is no reason,
For you to know, the fixed year and season.

"And you will be witness, in Jerusalem,
Judea, and Samaria, and all other nations."

Then He opened their minds to understand,
The scripture He said to them,

"That the Christ, the Messiah, should suffer, and be crucified,
And on the third day, from the dead, He would rise.

"And repentance and forgiveness of sins, will be preached in His name,
Among all nations, beginning with Jerusalem.

"And behold, I am sending forth the promise of My Father,
Stay in the city, until you are endued with power."

And He led them out, as far as Bethany,
And He lifted up His hands, and blessed them.

And it came to pass, while He was blessing them,
He left them, and was taken up into heaven.

And they all worshipped Him,
And returned to wait in Jerusalem.

Peter, James, John, and Andrew,
Philip, Thomas and Bartholomew,

Matthew, James, the son of Alphaeus,
Simon the zealot, Judas the brother of James, and the one chosen by lot,
Matthias.

CHAPTER 21
THE HOLY SPIRIT

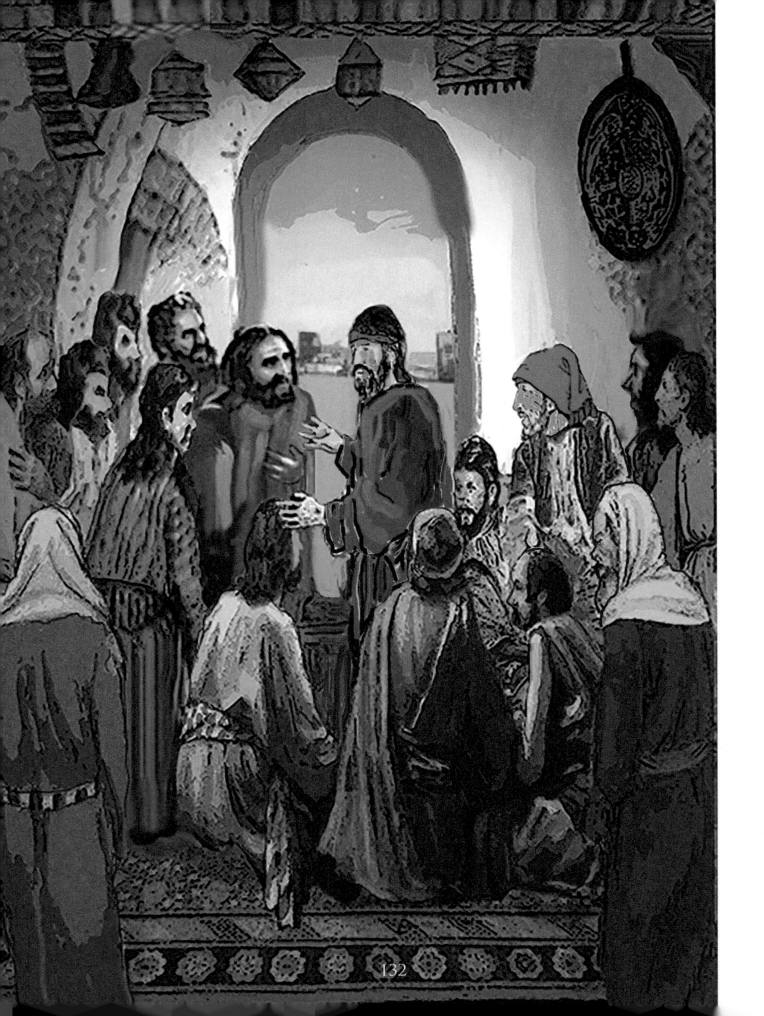

Then, there was again the twelve,
All are joined together, constantly in prayer.

And when the day of Pentecost, had finally come,
There were one hundred and twenty, in the upper room.

When suddenly the sound, of a violent wind blowing,
It came from heaven, and filled all the house, where they were sitting.

They saw what seemed to be, tongues of fire,
And all were filled with the Holy Spirit, and power.

Now, there were staying, in Jerusalem,
God fearing Jews, from every nation, under heaven.

When they heard, this sound,
Bewildered, all gathered around.

And they were amazed, and marveled saying,
"Are not all these who speak, Galileans?

"Then how is it that each of us hear, in his own tongue,
In his own language, and dialect wherein we were born?

"Parthians, Medes, and Elamites; residents of Mesopotamia,
Judea and Capadocia, Pontus and Asia,

"Phrygia, Pamphylia, Egypt, and the parts of Libya near Cyrene;
Visitors from Rome both Jews and proselytes; Arabs and Cretans.

"We hear them declaring,
The wonders of God saying."

And all were beside themselves, with amazement,
Greatly perplexed, puzzled, and bewildered, saying, "What meaneth this?"

But others made fun, they mocked and chimed,
"These men are simply drunk, and full of new wine."

Then Peter, stood up with the eleven,
Raised his voice, and declared to them:

"Fellow Jews, and all who live in Jerusalem,
Let me explain this to you, carefully listen.

"For these men are not drunk as you're imagining,
Seeing it is only nine in the morning.

"For this is what was told,
By the prophet Joel:

" 'In the last day, God says,
I will pour out my Spirit on all man.

" 'Your sons and daughters will prophesy, and visions by young men,
And your old men will dream dreams, again and again.

" 'Even on my servants men and women,
I will pour forth my Spirit in those days on them.

" 'I will show wonders in heavens above,
And signs and fire and billow of smoke.

" 'The sun will be turned to darkness, and the moon into blood,
Before the coming of the great, and glorious day of the Lord.'

"Men of Israel, listen to this,
He is the one, Jesus of Nazareth.

"Approved of God among you by signs, wonders and miracles,
Which God performed through Him, you know yourself.

"This Jesus, over to you by God He was handed,
Taken, and by lawless wicked hands have crucified and slandered.

"But God from the dead, raised Him up again,
Because death and the grave, could not hold Him.

"Therefore let all know, beyond all doubt,
God has made Him, both Lord and Christ.

"This Jesus, the Messiah,
Whom you crucified."

Now when they heard this, they were pierced to the heart,
Said to Peter, "What shall we do, where do we start?"

And Peter replied, "Repent, change your heart, your view,
Accept the will of God and be made new.

"Be baptized every one of you, in Jesus name, for the forgiveness and release from your sins,
And you will receive the Holy Spirit my friend.

"As many as the Lord, to Himself He will call,
For the promise is to you, and your children, and all that are afar."

And with many other words, he testified, and exhorted them saying,
"Save yourself from the crooked, perverse, wicked, unjust generation."

Therefore those who accepted, and welcomed his message,
Were baptized and about three thousand souls were added.

CHAPTER 22
MULTITUDE

They devoted themselves, to the apostle's teaching,
And to fellowship, to breaking bread, and to praying.

And everyone kept feeling a sense of great awe,
And many wondrous and miraculous signs were done by the apostles.

All the believers were together, and had everything in common,
Selling their possessions and goods they gave to anyone, as he had need for them.

They broke bread in their homes, and all together with glad hearts,
Every day they continued to meet together in the temple court.

Constantly praising God, and being in favor, and good will with all people,
And the Lord kept adding to their number daily, those that were being saved.

And the church was spirit filled and joyful,
Because its soul focus was on Jesus.

DEDICATION

I would like to dedicate this book to my daughters Shannon and Jody and to their husbands, Eric and Kyle, to the grandchildren Alex, Olivia, Sophia, Mia Jo, and Allia. Thanks to the crew at Hardee's (920 NW Broad St., Murfreesboro, TN) who graciously allowed me to work on this and similar projects for over ten years. Because of additional morning time needed, I finished "The Christmas Story Told In All Seasons" at McDonalds (1106 Memorial Blvd. and 337 Memorial Blvd., Murfreesboro, TN). I'd like to thank that crew also. And to all the Chick-fil-A's that honor the Lord's day. Also, special thanks to "The Christmas Story Told In All Seasons" Illustrator, Natalie Marion; and the two that aided greatly in the completion of this work Denise Pope and Anthony Gilkes. I applaud you all.

Love in Christ

CPSIA information can be obtained
at www.ICGtesting.com
Printed in the USA
LVOW02*1415190516

488909LV00002B/3/P

Subtraction Action

Written and illustrated by Loreen Leedy

Holiday House • New York

The author would like to thank Professor Donna R. Strand
from the School of Education, Baruch College,
City University of New York, for her assistance.

Our Subtraction Stories

4 - 3 by Sadie

I had four pencils.
The pencil sharpener ate three of them.
I have one pencil left.
4 - 3 = 1

8 − 8 by Otto

My mom baked eight cookies.
I ate all of them.
There were zero cookies left.
8 − 8 = 0

12 - 7 by Fay

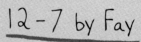

Our team scored twelve points.
Their team scored seven points.
We won by five points!
12 - 7 = 5

CONTENTS

9 - 7 by Tally

I had nine old toys.
I sold seven at a garage sale.
I had two toys left.
9 - 7 = 2

10 - 6 by Ginger

I grew ten big tomatoes.
I gave six of them away.
I had four tomatoes left.
10 - 6 = 4

What's the Difference?

Miss Prime showed her class a sign, a book, and a piece of paper.

7

What is the missing number?
$$7 - \underline{} = 2 \qquad \underline{} - 4 = 1$$

Answers: page 32

LeSS IS LeSS

13

A popular event at the school fair was the obstacle course.

START

FINISH

MinuS MaGic

Miss Prime put on a magic show at the school fair.

For my next trick, I'll subtract two of these seven balloon animals.

I'll just say the magic words: **minus two!**

23

Popcorn

Candy Apples

$1.00

$1.00

Do we get to eat the leftovers?

Tally had ten bags of popcorn and sold six. Otto had eight candy apples and sold three. Who had the least left over? Answer: page 32

NoThinG to LoSE

Sadie was determined to win a big, fuzzy stuffed bear.

30

How can you write Sadie's score as a subtraction equation?

Answer: page 32

31

Answers

page 6: The equation should read $9-6=3$ or $9-3=6$.

page 9: The missing number is five.
$7-\underline{5}=2$ $\underline{5}-4=1$

page 13: The difference between ten and five is five. $10-5=5$

page 19: Fay subtracted five seconds from the original time. $30-25=5$ Fay subtracted one second from Chester's time. $26-25=1$

page 24: I am the number nine. $20-11=9$

page 28: Tally had the least left over, because $10-6=4$ bags of popcorn and $8-3=5$ candy apples.

page 31: Sadie's score: $10-5-3-2=0$